BAAS Pamphlets in A

THE PEOPLE'S AMERICAN REVOLUTION

EDWARD COUNTRYMAN

British Association for American Studies

First published 1983

© British Association for American Studies, 1983
ISBN 0 946488 03 7

All rights reserved. No part of this pamphlet may be reproduced in any form or by any electronic or mechanical means, including information storage and retrieval systems, without permission in writing from the publisher, except by a reviewer who may quote brief passages in a review.

The publication of a pamphlet by the British Association for American Studies does not necessarily imply the Association's official approbation of the opinions expressed therein.

ACKNOWLEDGEMENTS

We are grateful to the Boston Museum of Fine Arts for the fine copy of John Singleton Copley's portrait of Paul Revere which is reproduced on page 13 by courtesy of the Museum (Gift of Joseph W., William B., and Edward H.R. Revere). The print of a popular convention on page 25 was kindly provided by, and appears by permission of, the American Antiquarian Society, Worcester, Massachusetts. The map on page 4 is taken from Jackson Turner Main, *The Sovereign States, 1775-1783* (copyright, 1973), with the permission of Franklin Watts, Inc., New York. The prints on the front cover and on pages 10, 15 and 35 are taken with approval from Alfred F. Young, ed., *The American Revolution: Explorations in the History of American Radicalism* (De Kalb, Ill.: Northern Illinois University Press), and **appear with the permission of the New York Historical Society, the Library of Congress, and the Pennsylvania Historical Society.**

Printed by Peterson Printers, 12 Laygate, South Shields, Tyne & Wear. Tel: (0632) 563493

Contents

1.	The Problem of the Revolution	5
2.	Americans of Many Kinds	11
3.	Resistance to Imperial Reform, 1765-1776	16
4.	The Political Revolution, 1774-1789	26
5.	Revolution and Transformation	33
	Appendix: 　The Artisans in the Revolution	37
	Guide to Further Reading	40
	Notes	44

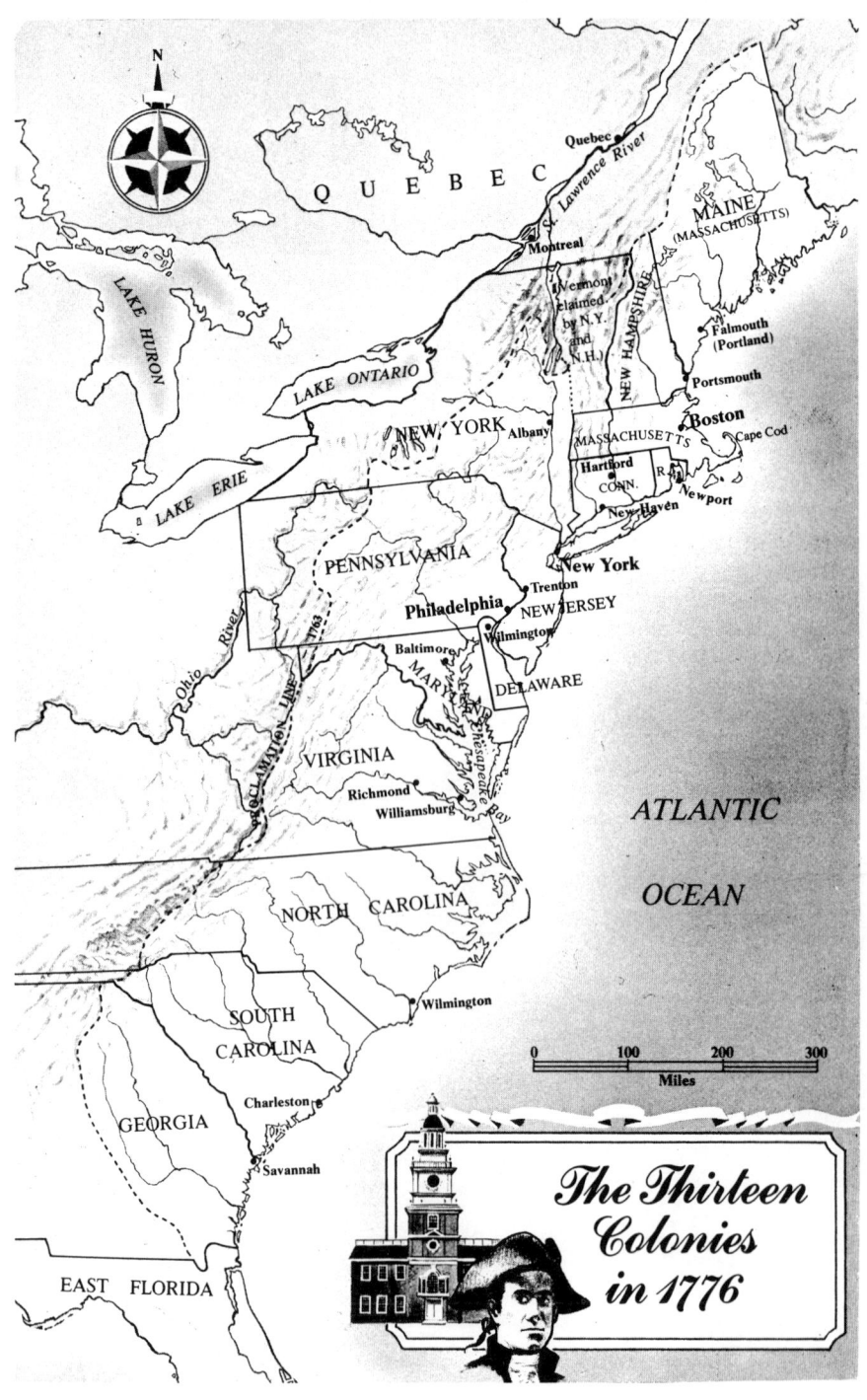

1: The Problem of the Revolution

What was the American Revolution? Was it simply the decision of the Thirteen Colonies to declare their independence? Or did it arise from the strains of war, as Britain struggled unsuccessfully to retain them? Did the Revolution lie in the replacement of monarchy by republican government? Was it brought about among a united people? Or did it pit different kinds of Americans against one another? Did it take place in the real world of social and political relationships, or in the realm of consciousness, mentality and ideology? Or was *the* Revolution no single one of these, but rather a grand transformation, binding many separate changes together?

The bare story seems simple enough: after 1763 Britain challenged the traditional autonomy of its colonies by introducing new policies of imperial reform and taxation; the colonies responded, nullifying first those policies and then their tie to Britain itself; finally, they created a republic where an empire had been. Yet the reality surrounding that story is complex indeed. Though analysts have tried for two full centuries to make sense of it, no single interpretation has ever won general acceptance. Among the earliest interpreters were the Revolution's participants and victims, for the aftermath of independence saw half-literate farmers, angry politicians, sophisticated intellectuals, and loyalist exiles all writing down their versions of what they had lived through. Yet for all that they had shared in its events, these men and women could not agree on what the Revolution had been. Writers of the time raised practically every question about the Revolution that academic historians have been arguing about since the writing of American history began. In particular, some contemporaries saw the Revolution as not merely a conflict between America and Britain, but a conflict — and transformation — within America itself.[1]

The earliest scholarly account of the Revolution — George Bancroft's *History of the United States*, written in the middle decades of the nineteenth century — established the academic tradition of seeing the Revolution as essentially a colonial struggle for independence. Bancroft was no professor; rather, he was a gentleman-scholar, a patriot, and a politician. He did his research carefully, but he wrote for, and reached, a general readership, using a colorful, impassioned prose that no modern academic would dare employ. For him the central story of the Revolution, and of all American history, was the rise of American liberty, a rise that was completed when the Founding Fathers wrote and implemented the Federal Constitution.[2] But despite his towering achievement, Bancroft's great work of Romantic "Whig" historiography inspired the first generation of professional historians to criticism rather than to emulation. Bancroft insisted that all American history pointed in one direction, but his successors began to consider the motives, the situations and the purposes of people for whom that direction had not been so clear.

The foremost such people during the Revolution, of course, were the British and the loyalists. Did Britain really intend to impose on the colonies a fearsome tyranny? Were Americans who opposed independence really that tyranny's crawling minions? The doubts that lie behind such questions began to seem plausible towards the end of the nineteenth century, and by World War I the intellectual climate had become ripe for a different view. That view first appeared in the work of Herbert Levi Osgood and George Louis Beer, and it culminated with that of Charles McLean Andrews and his many doctoral students, most notably Lawrence Henry Gipson.[3] These writers explored the problems that were faced by British statesmen, and they wrote with sympathy of what the loyalists endured. Unimpressed by the claim that Britain planned tyranny, many of them conceived the Revolution as simply a rash upsurge by colonists too small-minded to perceive the problems as men with an imperial viewpoint saw them. In their work the colonial movement became little more than a matter of selfish unwillingness to accept responsibilities. The policy changes that ignited the Revolution grew, they argued, not from a malevolent conspiracy but rather from the fact that in 1763, when those changes began, Britain stood exhausted from its long struggle with France. Since no one had gained more from British victory in that struggle than the colonists, who at last were free of the fear that the French would bring war to them from the west and north, it seemed only fitting that they should pay some of the cost. It was for that reason, wrote these "Imperial" scholars, that Britain attempted to tax them by the Sugar Act (1764), the Stamp Act (1765), and the Townshend Acts (1767). When the colonists resisted these measures, such writers maintained, it was simply for the sake of avoiding their just obligations.

While these scholars were denigrating the notion that the Revolution was a high-minded struggle for liberty against tyranny, others were challenging the idea that it was the movement of a united people. Such "Progressive" writers as Carl Becker, Charles A. Beard and the elder Arthur Schlesinger worked from a position of sympathy for ordinary men and women. In their dissections of the dynamics of the independence movement they found not broad agreement but rather dispute, conflict and manipulation. Becker summed up their approach when he argued in his 1909 study of the province of New York that the Revolution was not just a struggle over home rule; it also turned on the question of who should rule at home.[4] The culmination of this tendency came in 1913 when Charles Beard took the Founding Fathers, the men who met in 1787 to write the United States Constitution, down from the pinnacle where they had stood for so long. Far from being the disinterested patriots Bancroft had made them, Beard maintained that they wrote the Constitution primarily to restore value to depreciated paper securities that they had bought up at cheap rates. These Revolutionary leaders sought little more than to make a killing for themselves.[5]

Underlying both the Imperial and the Progressive interpretations lay a deep skepticism about the pieties of nineteenth-century American life. That such skepticism should have developed is not surprising. The last decades of the nineteenth century and the first years of the twentieth, when these scholars wrote, saw America and Britain moving ever closer in terms of world politics. They saw the United States itself becoming an imperialist power. They saw its citizens moving ever farther apart in terms of their dealings with one another. Yet the new historians based their accounts on massive research as well as on questions shaped in their own times. Their goal was to deepen understanding of the past, not simply to score polemical points.

But just as the broad generalizations of a Bancroft provoked pointed challenges, so did those of Beard and Becker themselves. By the middle of this century, in the atmosphere of national unity generated by World War II and the Cold War, historians were mounting a merciless attack on the Progressive framework. One of the central Progressive tenets had been that in early America a privileged elite had been pitted against a disenfranchised mass. Beginning in 1955, however, Robert E. Brown and B. Katherine Brown devoted study after study to a refutation of that argument.[6] Both the quantitative methods they used and the questions they asked have generated fierce debate, but it is now generally agreed that, in spite of property requirements, in most colonies probably a majority of adult, white males possessed the right to vote. At the same time, Forrest McDonald was arraying a massive amount of data to demonstrate that how those involved in approving the Constitution stood on the issue had nothing to do with whether they would gain from a rise in the value of depreciated securities.[7]

Brown and McDonald made possible a return to the nineteenth-century idea that Revolutionary Americans had been an undifferentiated, united people. The way to a fresh assertion of that proposition lay in the close attention that other historians had already begun to pay to the sheer wordiness of the Revolution's makers. They had poured out endless letters, pamphlets, essays, songs and broadsides, but neither historians concerned to explore internal conflict nor historians writing from the point of view of British officials had taken that outpouring very seriously. Becker, for instance, maintained in his study of *The Declaration of Independence* (1922) that the Revolutionaries had simply taken up one intellectual position after another as it suited their needs.[8]

But in 1948 Edmund S. Morgan advanced the argument that during the debates over the Stamp and Townshend Acts "official" colonial spokesmen maintained a coherent and unchanging position on the relationship of the colonies to Parliament. Morgan's thesis was that they took their ideas seriously and acted on the basis of them. It provided a starting point from which a new interpretive framework could take shape.[9] For a host of writers who have followed him, the prime problem to be considered has been Anglo-American "Whiggery," the political culture and political language of the era. Whiggery insisted that an eternal conflict existed between the principle of power and the principle of liberty, and that constant vigilance was needed if liberty were not to be lost. It equated liberty with government under laws made by parliamentary institutions, and it maintained that the British constitution, with its balance of Crown, Lords and Commons, provided the best means of making liberty secure. Many historians — including, among others, Clinton Rossiter, Douglass Adair, Cecelia Kenyon, and J.G.A. Pocock — have described Whiggery as an intellectual structure powerful enough to explain the Revolution by itself. With roots deep in traditions that reached back to medieval England and Renaissance Italy, that culture preconditioned its adherents to perceive tyranny behind any move to increase any government's strength. Whatever the British intended, it was less important than what the Americans understood by it.[10]

Admittedly, some of these writers, notably Gordon Wood, have demonstrated how the Revolution's intellectuals used the language of Whiggery to argue out their differences, and he and Pauline Maier have shown much interest in street radicals, crowd action and popular upheaval.[11] But, for the most part, all of these historians have been more concerned with a universe of discourse that the whole Revolutionary generation shared than with any social element — class, region, race, gender, religion — that set its members apart. Bernard Bailyn, in particular, has given classic expression to this approach, which has so much in common with that of Bancroft a full century earlier: once more the Revolution has become a struggle to preserve liberty, a struggle which in the end transformed traditional institutions and established American republicanism and, in time, democracy. Perhaps what most clearly distinguishes these modern historians from Bancroft is their awareness of how immensely ironic history can be, as people who set out to do one thing find themselves accomplishing something very different.[12]

But throughout the 1950s and the early 1960s writers such as Merrill Jensen and Jackson Turner Main kept alive the questions that the Progressive historians had elaborated. In Jensen's analyses of the Articles of Confederation, the postwar years, and the coming of the Revolution and in Main's many books on early American society and politics, divisive social experience, not shared values, remained the key to understanding.[13] A vigorous reinvestigation of that approach began in the late 1960s and is still underway, and it owes a great deal to the example of Jensen and Main. But this most recent writing has also been influenced by two other stimuli, one political, the other academic. The generation of historians who have produced it came to maturity as the United States experienced refusal by blacks to tolerate any longer the conditions white America had imposed on them. These historians lived through the war in Southeast Asia and the movement against it, and they saw the birth of new consciousness among such groups as women, homosexuals and Native Americans. Is it surprising that many of them are sensitive to questions of conflict and upheaval in a way that another generation might not have been? The other influence, of tremendous importance for the formation of historical concepts and the development of research methods, has been the work of such non-Americanists as George Rudé, Albert Soboul, E.J. Hobsbawm and E.P. Thompson. Their studies of English and European crowd action, class formation and popular culture have provoked many investigations of American material framed in similar terms. American historians like Gary B. Nash and Rhys Isaac, among others,[14] have argued that the Revolution was driven by a popular radicalism which was only partially connected with the intellectual world of Whiggery. They have maintained that as that radicalism worked itself out it transformed aspect after aspect of the lives of Revolutionary Americans. They have held that that transformation affected different kinds of Americans — farmers, artisans, merchants, women, blacks — in different ways and that it gave people who were otherwise powerless a chance to intervene in historic events on their own. These studies have insisted, although in a way quite different from that of the Progressive writers, that the Revolution was a time when Americans disputed among themselves over fundamental questions.

The aim of this pamphlet is *not* to present a synthesis of all these contrasting approaches to the Revolution, but to outline and explain the general understanding of that phenomenon that emerges from the work of the younger, more "radical," perhaps "neo-Progressive," historians. By no means would all of them agree with the views expressed here, and I do not interpret their work as the authors themselves would choose; inevitably this is the personal view of one historian of a "radical" persuasion, who might well be accused of trying to extend to the whole country the conclusions of his own work on New York, the province which in an earlier generation had sustained Becker's views.[15] Yet the fact remains that the most recent writing has brought forward much new material and many important perspectives which tend to modify the "ideological" interpretation of Bailyn, Wood and other "neo-Whigs." In particular, while students of the Whig beliefs and attitudes of the Revolutionary generation recognise that the Revolution transformed the American polity in subtle and unsuspected ways, more recent, "radical" writing has insisted that this was no mere accident. Rather, it was the necessary consequence of the upsurge of popular involvement in the Revolution — on the part of people who had not normally exercised influence or participated in decision-making in the various societies and polities of colonial America.

The colonial farmer at the plough, as depicted on the title page of John Tobler's Almanack, *published in by Christopher Sower at Germantown, Pennsylvania, between 1749 and 1759 (Library of Congress).*

2: Americans of Many Kinds

There were no "colonists" or "Americans" in 1763. Instead, there were people of one empire and of many colonies. People thought of themselves in terms of their provinces, or perhaps as Britons overseas, but no United States existed. The thirteen provinces that rebelled — and the many such as Nova Scotia, Quebec and Jamaica that did not — were more than just administrative units. Each was a separate political society. Colonies and mother country alike shared the heritage of the English Whig settlement, which had established the principle that power was jointly held by the Crown, the House of Lords and the House of Commons. In the colonies a governor stood in place of the King, a council in place of the Lords and, as far as the colonists were concerned, a local assembly in place of the Commons. But political practices varied from province to province. In Massachusetts a town meeting might well resolve a set of direct instructions for the town's delegate to the provincial assembly. In Virginia there were no towns to meet, and if people wanted something from the government they expressed their desires deferentially, informally and as individuals. New Yorkers and Pennsylvanians were used to their leaders openly competing for support; South Carolinians were famous for their harmony. In Virginia a well-defined ruling class wielded power in a manner that most other whites accepted. In neighboring North Carolina, no real planter class had appeared and those who tried to rule found that others gave them little respect.[16]

The colonies were diverse socially as well. South Carolina had so many blacks that it was "more like a negro country"; two of every five Virginians were likewise black and enslaved. In those two provinces productive work meant black labor to raise staple crops like tobacco, rice and indigo for export. In Georgia and North Carolina there were far fewer blacks; the plantation system had not yet triumphed, and most whites lived as small farmers, remote from the Atlantic market. In northern Virginia and southern Maryland tobacco culture shaded off into wheat raising, and from there north to New York the main export was grain. In New Jersey and Pennsylvania the grain was raised largely by small freehold farmers, but a sizable proportion of New York's crop was grown by white tenants on great estates. Some of those estates faintly reflected the heritage of European feudalism. Except for New Hampshire timber and Connecticut horses, the small freehold farms of New England exported little in the way of agricultural goods; indeed, the region had to import a good proportion of its food.[17]

The colonies existed within a larger world. In some ways their societies looked very much like those to be found elsewhere, and as they grew in population and wealth, that became more and more the case. There were colonials who had experienced that larger world directly, before migration or on journeys to England and Europe. There were others who lived with memories of Europe — or Africa — passed down from their parents and grandparents. For some, the world elsewhere provided a model of civilization to be emulated; for others, it was a model of corruption to be shunned. There were colonists who knew that the Spanish-American provinces to the south did not enjoy the British political tradition, and some may have known that in Mexico City, as in Paris or London, there were extremes of wealth and poverty not to be found in British America. But what counted most in the colonists' day-to-day lives were the relationships within which they lived with one another.

Those relationships were shaped by an absence, save in the case of slave and free, of formally defined, legally established social positions. But black slavery, which was unique to the Americas, had been shaped in the first place by the demands of a market system that centered on western Europe and that stretched across half the world. That same market system affected the relationships of all North Americans, although in different ways.

The major cities, Charleston, Philadelphia, New York, Newport and Boston, all had thriving communities of merchants. Some were agents of British and European trading houses, but others bought and sold up and down the Atlantic coast and into the Caribbean. Not a few prospered on the slave trade. Some of these merchants had prominent British connections and vast fortunes; £50,000 sterling was not uncommon in New York. Many others operated on a much smaller scale, not even bearing the titles — Esq., Gent., Mr. — that signified gentility in colonial society. Such men lived close to the artisan communities in each of the cities. An artisan, or "mechanic," might be a journeyman baker or a wealthy master printer with many employees, but he worked with his hands. John Singleton Copley's well-known portrait of Paul Revere *(see opposite)* illustrates the pride artisans could take in themselves. Revere posed for it not in Sunday best but in his work clothes, with his tools and a silver teapot of his making in front of him. But at best such men were only half-inside the political community, voters and minor office-holders but never wielders of power. Below the artisans, and their journeymen and apprentices, were laborers and servants, some of them white, some black, some free, some bound servants, some slaves. At every social level there were some women who acted independently, running trading houses and shops or simply working on their own. But most women knew little of the world of affairs, and most thought their sex almost automatically disqualified them from any social role beyond that of "good wives."[18] The social relationships of the largest cities provided a model for lesser places, such as Salem, Massachusetts, or

Paul Revere, by John Singleton Copley.
Courtesy, Museum of Fine Arts, Boston.
Gift of Joseph W., William B., and Edward H.R. Revere

Revere was the Boston silversmith who rode to Lexington and Concord in April, 1775, with the news that British troops were on their way to seize stores hidden there. Henry Wadsworth Longfellow's nineteenth-century poem "The Midnight Ride of Paul Revere" immortalized Revere's adventure. But the silversmith's real importance lies in the way that he represents the many articulate, self-confident artisans who plunged into Revolutionary politics.

Baltimore, Maryland. In Philadelphia, New York and Boston, at least, the eighteenth century saw a marked trend towards the concentration of wealth and towards the growth of a group of marginal and really poor people.[19]

In the countryside, too, people's lives varied widely. A South Carolina or a Virginia planter or the holder of a New York estate might have a fortune in excess of £100,000. A slave had nothing. A tenant or a small farmer might have a leasehold or a freehold worth several hundred pounds. In some places, such as tidewater Virginia or the New York estates, great wealth and modest means might exist side by side. But the holders of South Carolina's great fortunes were to be found in the lowlands, separated by many miles from small farmers in the backcountry. In New York a tenant on the east bank of the Hudson and a freeholder on the west bank might pay roughly equal taxes. But the tenant lived on land that belonged to someone of a wholly different order and the freeholder in a community in which no great fortune existed.

Similar communities, roughly egalitarian, were to be found in New England. They were densely organized around networks of church, town meeting and family. They did include people who were well off and people who were really poor, but even the "river gods" of the Connecticut Valley held nothing like the fortunes of New York landlords or Virginia planters. Some towns in eastern New England were becoming seriously overcrowded by mid-century, with disease on the increase, life expectancy falling, and young adults finding themselves compelled to migrate. Many of those migrants went either north, towards the Green Mountain region that New York, Massachusetts and New Hampshire all claimed, or west, towards the ill-defined borderland that separated New York from Massachusetts.[20] Throughout the interior of New England and the middle colonies and the backcountry of the South there were people whose lives were touched but little by the long-distance and impersonal relationships of the Atlantic market. Instead, they lived within networks of exchange and obligation that were local and often non-monetary. They experienced the world very differently from people whose crops and goods were destined for sale far away.

Relationships among these different people were complex and tangled. Everywhere the realm of high power was the preserve of the elite. But what marked an elite off, how its members conceived of themselves, and how they dealt with "lesser" people varied. Throughout the colonies it was the votes of ordinary men that gave great men their political power. But in rural New England they enjoyed that power within organic communities. New York landlords enjoyed it because they could command the suffrage of their tenants. Virginia planters enjoyed it within an elaborate pattern of ritual, *bonhomie* and deference that simultaneously permitted *politesse* and self-assertion, market relations and the image of a bucolic idyll, planter power and cross-class camaraderie.

The overall process of the Revolution would be worked out within these sometimes tense, sometimes relaxed, sometimes commercial, sometimes organic, sometimes hierarchical, sometimes consensual relationships. It would see the making and unmaking of a series of political coalitions, each structured around both the great issues of the day and the local concerns of particular groups and communities. That process would fundamentally alter the ways in which people dealt with one another. In no place would the Americans of 1790 live in quite the same way as had the colonists of 1760.

An American crowd in action. This forceful woodcut shows a demonstration in Boston in February, 1770. The crowd is expressing its anger towards a customs informer, an anger increased by the informer's shooting of an eleven year old boy. The smoking gun that extends from the central house represents the shot that killed him. A month later five more Bostonians would be killed when British troops opened fire on another crowd. From The Life and Humble Confessions of Richardson, The Informer *(Pennsylvania Historical Society).*

3: Resistance to Imperial Reform, 1765-1776

The policy changes that Britain began to make in 1763 dealt with the administration and the finance of the empire. The prime purpose of the empire had always been to orient the wealth of the colonies for Britain's benefit, and since the time of Oliver Cromwell a piecemeal series of laws had been enacted to achieve that goal. These laws established a "Navigation System" that imposed obligations on the colonies but provided significant benefits in return. Colonial commerce was restricted to British vessels, but ships of American construction counted as British and a flourishing ship-building industry resulted. Some crops, such as tobacco, rice and indigo, were restricted to the British market, but there they generally found ready sale, in some cases with direct support from the British government. There were legal restrictions on what the colonists might produce, and there were severe duties on goods imported from outside the empire. All of these elements of the Navigation System simply reflected the fact that the colonies lay on the periphery of an economic structure over which they had no real control. They existed, in theory and in many ways in reality, not for their own sakes but to serve the needs of metropolitan Britain. There were elements in their developing societies, such as staple-crop production and unfree labor, that they shared with other parts of the eighteenth-century periphery, including eastern Europe, South America and the Caribbean. It may be that had independence not happened in the way it did North America's future would have been marked by dependency and underdevelopment instead of by the dynamic autonomy that the nineteenth-century United States was to enjoy. But there is no denying that prior to 1763 the system did confer important benefits at little perceived cost. The "enumerated goods" had a good market, the hat and iron industries flourished despite the restrictions of the Iron Act and the Hat Act, and the duties on foreign imports were easily evaded. Years of "salutary neglect" had enabled the colonists to become accustomed to being effectively autonomous. The practices of merchants who traded where and as they thought best and of politicians who acted as if a provincial assembly was the equivalent of the House of Commons both reflected colonials' belief that they ran their own lives.[21]

After 1763, however, the British government challenged that belief, again and again. The end in that year of the "Great War for Empire" (or Seven Years War) saw British politicians determined to assert the mother country's superiority, both as a matter of principle and as a matter of direct interest. They embarked on a program of policy changes, aimed at establishing that superiority. They enforced laws that had been left lax; they created an American customs service; they demanded that colonial assemblies vote funds to support regular troops; most of all, they taxed. The Stamp Act of 1765, the Townshend Taxes of 1767 and the Tea Affair of 1773 all grew out of British conviction that Parliament had the power to tax the colonists directly, that it represented and ruled them just as much as it did Britons at home.

The movement that opposed those taxes marked the first stage in the development of the Revolution's popular radicalism. Ordinary people became involved for many different reasons, as colonists of different sorts came to the conclusion that great events were making their lives intolerable. This movement deserves to be called radical for three different reasons. First, it generated not simply discussion about British policies that Americans disliked but also direct action strong enough to frustrate those policies and make them unworkable. Second, it brought to political consciousness large groups of people who previously had stayed out of public affairs. Third, it generated political formations that were without precedent in colonial life. The eventual result was a situation in which the old institutions of power could no longer endure.

Radical opposition developed not as a single united movement but rather as a series of coalitions. The coalition that prevented the implementation of the Stamp Act in 1765 was not the same as the coalition that achieved independence in 1776. Nor was either the same as the coalition behind the Federal Constitution in 1787. To simply speak of "Americans" or of "colonists" will not do. Rather, we must understand each stage of the Revolution in terms of the precise combination of groups, interests and individuals that took a stance in the political arena. We cannot understand how each coalition developed unless we understand why and how its separate elements involved themselves.

The initial strength came from two sources. One was the political elites, gathered in institutions like Virginia's House of Burgesses. That the elites had reason to be disturbed is clear: Parliament's assertion of its might threatened their own power. Moreover, within their Whig world-view, the imposition of British policy without going through the ritual of consent by a representative assembly was the first step to tyranny. British spokesmen argued that such consent had been given, in Parliament, but the colonial elite argued forcefully that they, not the House of Commons, represented the people of the colonies. They produced incisive pamphlets; their assemblies passed resounding resolutions; they used their connections to bring pressure in Britain itself. This leadership by the most prominent men and the leading institutions of colonial society was important, for it helped to legitimate colonial anger in the language of high principle. But equally important was the second source of opposition, which expressed itself not so much in words as in the direct, militant action of ordinary people. Without that direct action the opposition to British policy would have come to nothing more than a debate. Popular involvement was what changed that debate to a movement.

The cardinal fact in the popular politics of the decade from the Stamp Act to Independence was crowd action. Between 1765 and 1775 crowds nullified the Stamp Act, frustrated the American Customs Commissioners, brawled with redcoats, and dumped tea into more than one harbor. They closed courts and tore down elegant houses. They broke jails open and stopped surveying parties and disrupted concerts. Some acted as extensions of the governments of their own communities, some in direct opposition to those governments, and some brought governments down. Some crowds were led by prominent men from outside their own ranks, but some brought forth their own leaders, out of the depths of obscurity.

Such crowd action was not new, nor was it mindless chaos. Mobs had long been a feature of eighteenth-century life, and they erupted within a framework of political economy and popular culture that governed how crowd members behaved and gave some forms of crowd action a quasi-institutional legitimacy. Traditional, pre-Revolutionary crowds often acted because the authorities could not: what, after all, was a sheriff's posse or a militia company or a volunteer fire company other than a crowd, drawn into ranks and given official standing? Sometimes pre-Revolutionary crowds acted to prevent an indiscriminate evil, such as smallpox contagion entering a community. But sometimes they defended the direct interests of their own members. Sometimes they did both. As Jesse Lemisch has argued, merchant seamen who rioted in Boston in 1747 against impressment into the British navy were saving Boston as a whole, for while a press was on boatmen would not bring in food and fuel and merchants could not put their ships to sea. But they were also saving themselves from the horrors of naval life, and in their own minds that was what counted most.[22]

Other crowds turned out because men outside their own ranks called them forth. Elections, especially in the middle colonies, frequently saw each side stationing its gangs of toughs at the polls. Sometimes crowds took direct action on matters of private property. Crowds never attacked the *principle* of private ownership, but they often acted on the belief that people besides the owner had a rightful say in how property might be used. The economic life of early American towns did not revolve around an unrestrained free market; rather, the towns were heirs to a long European tradition that a community might interfere in property's use for the sake of the general welfare. That tradition took one form in New York and Philadelphia, where the authorities established controlled markets in which important commodities had to be sold. It took another in Boston, where in 1737 a crowd tore down the building erected for just such a market. But the basic point was clear: the right to a supply of necessities like bread, salt and firewood was more important than the right of a merchant dealing in them to find his profit where he could. Both in Europe and in America ordinary people enforced that tradition if the authorities did not. This traditional "corporatism" underlay a great deal of the crowd action that America experienced between 1760 and 1780.[23]

The crowds of the countryside present still more complexities. Pennsylvania settlers rose in 1763, doing fearful injury to peaceful Indians and then marching on Philadelphia. This "march of the Paxton Boys" subsided quickly, but elsewhere rural movements proved durable, lasting in some cases for years. In the Green Mountains, on the east bank of the Hudson River and in central New Jersey, small farmers rose over who would hold the land and how it would be developed. In both Carolinas movements of upland "Regulators" challenged the policies and the power of provincial governments that were based in the lowlands. When country people rose, the authorities took them seriously, condemning their leaders to death without trial and calling out the militia and regular British troops to put them down.[24]

Late colonial America, in other words, was a turbulent, unstable place, where direct action could both extend and frustrate the power of government. Crowd action could spring from the solidarity of people whose communities were under threat, but it could also express the hostility of people whose interests clashed. But that was true of virtually the whole Atlantic world at the time. What turned the crowds of North America from recognized elements in that world into a revolutionary force, able to turn a part of it upside down?

The answer is that day-to-day grievances meshed with imperial issues to create a general crisis, a process fostered by the group of self-conscious radicals that emerged under the name Sons of Liberty. Their achievement was to create a militant, disciplined American movement capable of directly opposing British policy and power. Who were they? What is the relationship between their militancy, domestic grievances, and the imperial issue?

Pauline Maier has shown how the Sons emerged at the time of the Stamp Act as an inter-colonial group.[25] Bent on militant opposition to British policy, they provided both geographical links between widely separated places and social links between the Whig elite and the plebs. Maier has argued convincingly that in their own eyes they were not tribunes of an oppressed people, bent on forcing the imperial issue for the sake of internal change. But she and others have also demonstrated that they were men of very specific sorts. Many were artisans, like Paul Revere in Boston or the instrument maker John Lamb in New York. Others were small-scale intercolonial merchants, such as the New York street leaders Isaac Sears and Alexander McDougall. Frequently they were men on the make: Sears was the son of an oyster catcher, McDougall of a milkman, Lamb of a convict servant. The Sons also attracted unhappy intellectuals, like the Harvard graduate Samuel Adams and the self-taught physician Thomas Young. Adams glowed with a vision of a Christian Sparta; Young preached an unabashed Deism: they knew that if they let themselves they could disagree on a great deal. But they shared an outrage towards the world they lived in, a closeness to ordinary people, and a delight in public action. Whatever they were, the Sons stood several rungs down the social ladder from the elite. They were literate enough and sophisticated enough to understand the arguments of a John Dickinson or the resolutions of a House of Burgesses. They were well enough off to have the time to sit in the gallery and watch the provincial assembly debate. But even their costume — long trousers and leather aprons rather than the knee-breeches and silk and velvet of the elite — marked them as of the people rather than of the "better sort."

How and on what terms the Sons and the members of the crowds dealt with one another varied. The "Loyal Nine," from whom the Sons in Boston emerged, used several means in 1765 to generate their town's resistance to the Stamp Act. As an early preparation, they contacted a cobbler named Ebenezer Mackintosh. Mackintosh was leader of one of the crowds that traditionally gathered on "Pope's Day," November 5, to build elaborate anti-Catholic effigies and sometimes to brawl. Now the Loyal Nine asked him to turn out his followers on a different, more immediate issue. On the day of the first rising the radicals acted out a dramatic open-air tableau to show all Bostonians how the Stamp Act would disrupt their lives. But these emergent Sons of Liberty insisted that their townsmen confine direct action to the imperial issue. Their *tableau vivant* of August 14 provoked an uprising in which a crowd sacked a building which Stamp Distributor Andrew Oliver was supposedly preparing to use as an office, and then Oliver's house. The Sons applauded. But when crowds gathered again on August 26 and destroyed the mansion of Lieutenant-Governor Thomas Hutchinson, the Sons joined the town's elite in a chorus of condemnation. Hutchinson, they believed, had nothing to do with the Stamp crisis. Their orientation came across clearly in their newspaper, *The Boston Gazette*. Throughout the late 1760s it was filled with angry, militant prose, but invariably it focused on the British issue, not on local concerns.

But in New York City the Sons acted differently. They showed no opposition at all in November 1765, when crowds sacked the mansion of a British officer and burned carriages and sleighs belonging to the lieutenant-governor. Early in 1766 Sons actually led a crowd that disrupted the first performance in a newly-opened theatre, driving out the patrons and the actors and then tearing the building down. *Their* newspaper, *The New York Journal*, carried essay after essay attacking the evils of high rents, rising prices and short employment. At the end of 1769 two New York Sons, Alexander McDougall and John Lamb, launched a campaign against the presence of British troops in the city. McDougall wrote a broadside accusing the provincial assembly of betraying New York by voting money for the troops' support; when the assembly imprisoned him for contempt, his associates dramatized his plight and made him a popular hero. But Lamb understood what made people angry. *His* broadside accused the off-duty troops of taking scarce jobs that New Yorkers needed, and it sparked off days of street violence.[26]

Never was there a single pattern: each group of Sons operated in its own way in its own community. But they did maintain contact, pledge mutual cooperation, and keep political consciousness high from the Stamp Act Crisis to the Coercive Acts of 1774. Maier's demonstration of how they did it forms one of the central statements in the present understanding of the Revolution.

But the Sons were a phenomenon of the cities and the large towns, and, at most, townspeople totalled less than five percent of the American population in 1775. Without massive rural involvement the American movement would have come to nothing. When and why did country people join in? As in the cities, local grievances, popular culture and the hard work of political organization all combined to make a movement.

Consider three places about which we know a fair amount, Massachusetts, New York and Virginia. In economic, cultural and even political terms they had little in common, and their Revolutionary experiences varied enormously. New England's synthesis was decaying rapidly by the third quarter of the century, with family, village and church no longer providing a cohesive social framework. Moreover, through the 1760s and early 1770s Governors Francis Bernard and Thomas Hutchinson tried to co-opt the village leaders who were elected to the provincial assembly by offering them posts as justices of the peace and ranking militia officers. Loyalism would not be an enormous problem in Massachusetts or the other New England provinces, but it would attract a disproportionate number of those leaders. Boston radicals set out to rouse rural Massachusetts opinion as early as 1768, when they called delegates from the towns to a provincial convention. Between 1772 and 1774 their committee of correspondence waged a ceaseless propaganda campaign in the hinterland, and by 1774 the entire province was a tinderbox. In the summer of that year angry farmers forcibly closed county courts and demanded the resignations of high officers. By the autumn those same farmers had begun gathering military stores and preparing for war, and on two occasions they spontaneously turned out by the tens of thousands in response to rumors of fighting near Boston. The first was a false alarm; the second, in April 1775, was the real thing.[27] Rural Massachusetts had entered the Revolution for many reasons. By 1774 its people were genuinely angry about what the British were doing in response to Boston's Tea Party. They said so repeatedly in the resolutions of their town meetings. But at the same time these farmers were fearful that they were on the point of losing their land and their way of life, for reasons only partly connected with the British issue. They were angry at local leaders who had let themselves be seduced by colonelcies and judgeships. Thus, when they closed the courts and humiliated the judges, sheriffs and royal councillors, they were protesting against more than the Massachusetts Government Act, by which Parliament had reorganized the province in the aftermath of the Tea Party. They were also striking at their own local elite, at the social trends for which it stood, and at the institutions through which it ruled.[28]

Rural New Yorkers were of at least three sorts. Some, near New York City, lived in stable, prosperous, market-oriented communities. Others, more remote, lived in communities that were almost as cohesive, but that were much less tied to the market. Still others lived on the great estates. These were anything but cohesive, and in 1766 they erupted in a massive rising that stretched from New York City to Albany. But all New Yorkers lived under a provincial government that was operating more and more on the principle of providing for the interests of men who actually held office. New York City radicals took much less interest in the countryside than did their Boston counterparts. The province's elite of merchants and landlords itself split open, and ordinary people went in four different directions. Almost unanimously the counties around New York City became loyalist. Overwhelmingly the yeoman counties on the west bank of the Hudson became Revolutionary. But after 1775 the counties of great estates on the east bank and in the Mohawk Valley broke into civil war, with some landlords and some tenants choosing each side. In the far north the Green Mountains, which Britain had formally awarded to New York in 1764, broke away to establish the separate state of Vermont.[29]

Virginia was different again. Though it was the most populous province it had no cities. It knew wealth and it knew poverty, but all its whites knew they were not black and understood the codes of behavior that made them in some ways an organic group. Nonetheless, problems were developing, and as in Massachusetts and New York, they involved relations between people who were privileged and people who were not. Evangelical religion was attracting humble Virginians away from planter Anglicanism, and some planters were disturbed enough by it to break up Methodist and Baptist meetings forcibly. The planters themselves were caught between a fascination with the glittering culture of metropolitan England and an awareness of their own provincialism. They were increasingly conscious, as well, of corruption and decay in their own ranks. The scandal in 1766 over illegal loans made by the provincial treasurer John Robinson was only one piece of evidence. When the Revolution came, Virginians did not launch an assault on the established political order, as Massachusetts farmers did. They did not divide in any serious way into rebels and loyalists, as rural New Yorkers did. Most of the elite chose independence, and most lesser whites followed them. As J.R. Pole has commented, Virginia's open, seemingly democratic state constitution of 1776 is a monument to the planters' confidence that they could continue to rule their world.[30]

Instead, as Rhys Isaac has forcefully argued, Virginia's tensions expressed themselves largely in religious and symbolic terms. The revival that lured poorer whites was not unique to Virginia, for in mid-century all of the colonies had been swept by a wave of evangelical fervor. So intense was it that it split Congregationalists and Presbyterians into antagonistic wings, gave new impetus to Baptists, and laid the basis for the eventual rise of Methodism. Everywhere it erupted this "Great Awakening" drew on social tensions, and frequently it spilled over into politics. Isaac has shown that in Virginia the demeanor and belief of the evangelicals challenged the whole synthesis of public display, hierarchy, *bonhomie*, individualism and racism that Virginia's planter class had painfully constructed. A writer using E.J. Hobsbawm's categories might describe these Baptists and Methodists as primitive rebels, using their austere and egalitarian religion to protest against the ostentation and the stratification of planter life. The planters met the challenge: the issue did not break Virginia apart. They did it not least by recruiting their humbler fellows into a Revolution that they, the planters, would lead. But ordinary white Virginians got involved on terms that they chose themselves, and in consequence they changed the tone of Virginia life. Revolutionary Virginia, like colonial Virginia, built its social life around ritual and drama, but its rituals were different. They stressed commitment to the cause and equality among the men who joined. When the planter elite gathered in a Revolutionary congress wearing not their traditional costumes but rather the hunting shirts of plain men, it signified their acceptance of change.[31]

REPRESENTATION of a COUNTY-CONVENTION for REDRESS of GRIEVANCES. of COURTS.

HOW blest is that INTERPRETER of Laws,
  Who rich and Poor make equal in a Cause!
Who dares with steady hand the Balance hold,
And ne'er inclines it to one Side for Gold;
Altho' in Rags, one Scale gives equal weight,
Against the gilded Trappings of the Great.
'Tis such alone deserves our just Applause,
And such alone gives Sanction to the LAWS.

Each of these patterns was unique, yet each represented the particular expression of larger developments. In most provinces backcountry social grievance burst in some way into political dispute. It took one form among the South Carolina Regulators, who demanded courts where there were none. It took another in North Carolina, where other Regulators challenged the rule of would-be grandees. In Maryland the planter class nearly lost its hold at independence in the face of widespread "disaffection" and outright popular loyalism. Tenant rebellion and loyalism in the Hudson Valley, land rioting in New Jersey, and the movement that freed Vermont from New York had a great deal in common. Independence in New England saw the flowering of evangelical sects as radical as any that had appeared during old England's "revolution of the saints" a century before.[32] Each of these developments took place in a particular society, but all fed into the way that Americans experienced their political Revolution.

FACING PAGE:
A Revolutionary convention in session.
This woodcut from a New England almanac presents an almost unique view of ordinary people making their Revolution. Popular conventions and committees provided the means by which Americans nullified British power and made independence possible. After 1776 people turned to them again and again to resolve the problems that independence itself brought. Courtesy of the American Antiquarian Society, Worcester, Massachusetts.

4: The Political Revolution, 1774-1789

In political terms *revolution* means rapid, fundamental change, as one set of power relationships and institutions collapses and another takes its place. That is why it is always wrong to use the word to describe a mere shift of ruling groups while institutions endure. On this count, the American Revolution seems problematical. The states look so similar to the provinces. The period seems one of simple, easy continuity, with change happening only when the break with Britain made it necessary.[33] But this was in fact far from the case.

Independence was achieved by gatherings that were wholly illegal from the standpoint of the old order. Popular committees at the level of towns and counties, conventions in the provinces, and the Continental Congress were revolutionary manifestations of the most fundamental sort. Between 1774 and 1776 they destroyed the old political order at every level, and brought direct involvement in politics to men who had never before experienced it. The Declaration of Independence, proclaimed by the Continental Congress, was the culmination of a process that began with the closing of the Massachusetts courts, organized by town committees. It was through these committees, conventions and congresses that the Revolution came to ordinary people and that ordinary people made their Revolution.

The committee movement had two sources. One was spontaneous and local, the other orchestrated and proto-national. In large communities and small, the aftermath of the Boston Tea Party, with the town's harbor closed and the government of Massachusetts reorganized, moved men to organize themselves so they could help. Sometimes the organizers were simply the old elite. In the Carolinas, as in Virginia, Whig gentlemen strove mightily to convince their humbler neighbors to overcome their doubts and fears and join in.[34] But in general where popular committees appeared "new men" did as well. Sometimes they were brought in to give the movement the broadest possible base; sometimes they pushed their own way forward in open conflict; sometimes their involvement sprang from a mixture of the two.

Richard Ryerson's study of the committee movement in Philadelphia shows how it brought disruption, mobilization, and transformation. Radical politics there resulted directly from the emergence of an organized, articulate mechanic class, and merchants hostile to Britain found themselves forced to enter into a series of coalitions with these men. The mechanics found their political forum in the committee, which, as time went on, came to be made up of men less and less characterized by property and prestige. The organization of committees created a situation of dual power, as they vied with the provincial government for authority and finally brought that government down in the summer of 1776. Ryerson links the internal disputes, the emergence of new men, and the politicization of day-to-day issues with the larger struggle for American freedom. Building a coalition whose members knew and expressed their own interests while they acted on the larger question was a "basic revolutionary process."[35]

The committee movement began with tens, perhaps hundreds, of separate local initiatives. But it gained continental scope and political force at two clearly visible points. In November 1774, the first Continental Congress called for "committees in County, City and Town" to enforce its economic boycott of Britain. Neither boycotts of British commerce nor committees to enforce them were new by this time, but previous committees had been picked by a town's merchants; now they would be picked at elections and mass meetings by the whole body of citizens. These committees had a mandate to interfere directly in economic life to enforce the boycott. They could, and did, order the seizure of goods imported in violation of it. They could, and did, hold up violators for public contempt and ostracism. The Continental Association, as the boycott was called, did more than resist Britain; it marked a long step towards the transformation of America.

With the outbreak of war in April 1775, community after community gathered to elect committees of safety able to meet the crisis. Committees that had consisted of four or five self-chosen men operating half in secret grew to memberships of thirty or more and began operating openly. In Albany County, New York, mass meetings early in May elected a committee of 153 members to replace one of perhaps fifteen. In New York City a committee of one hundred men was elected after days of tumult in which Sons of Liberty broke open the town arsenal and took control of the streets.[36]

The first task of the committees of safety was to organize for war. The need was for a popular army that could defend the local community and that could go, if need be, to Massachusetts, where half-organized farmers confronted General Thomas Gage and the only powerful British force in America. As soon as it formed, the Albany committee of safety asked the mayor to organize a "burgher's watch," and when he refused established one itself. In Philadelphia, as in Virginia, the costume of the Revolutionary militia became an emblem of much larger tensions, for ordinary militiamen insisted that a plain hunting shirt would do for officers and men alike. They raised the issue through their committee of privates, whose very name betokened what was underway. By organizing those militia units and by assembling supplies and raising finance for them, the committees were turning themselves into a counter-government. They began to meet not in taverns or private homes but in their own "committee chambers." They established jails for the Revolution's enemies, appointed officials to carry out their orders, and summoned the citizens to public meetings which they expected everyone to attend. As early as the summer of 1775 local government could do little unless the committee agreed and by 1776 the committees were wielding all power.[37]

The committees were radical both because they developed and operated outside the old framework of legality and because of the way they brought new men into public life. Farmers, small merchants and artisans suddenly found themselves at the center of affairs. What their involvement could lead to was shown most clearly in Philadelphia in 1776. When Tom Paine wrote and published *Common Sense* he made himself the voice of the small people whom the Revolution had brought into politics. Eschewing ornate references and classical quotations, he slashed through the rationale of monarchy. He likewise abandoned traditional Whig politics, with its careful balance of the principles of monarchy, aristocracy, and democracy. Paine called for the establishment of a simple republic, with direct, responsive institutions, and throughout the continent people agreed that he had spoken for them. In Pennsylvania such men, Philadelphia artisans and backcountry farmers alike, joined together to write a radical democratic state constitution that provided no governorship and no upper house. By annual elections, by simple requirements for office, and by requiring that laws be submitted to the people before they were finally enacted, the Pennsylvania constitution came close to institutionalizing the massive involvement that the committee movement had generated.[38]

Nor were Pennsylvanians alone. The Green Mountain rebels, struggling simultaneously against Britain and against New York, took the Pennsylvania constitution as a model for their own. Anonymous writers in Massachusetts began to produce pamphlets bearing titles such as *The People the Best Governors*. Mechanics in New York City, hearing in May 1776 that a new state constitution was to be written, sent a bold message to their "elected delegates," demanding that before going into effect it be submitted to the people. But, perhaps more indicative of where they stood, they demanded that *any* constitution leave the citizens free to recreate their revolutionary committees at any time and for any reason they might choose.[39]

Nor did the movement stop at the point of independence. Rather, it persisted in places as late as 1778, and in 1779 popular pressure revived it all over the Northern states. Committees persisted and were revived because ordinary people saw in them the best means of dealing with the economic and social distress that the War of

Independence brought. The war's demands were severe: three armies, American, British and French, competed for scarce supplies; continental and state currency depreciated to the point of worthlessness; refugees from areas of battle and zones of British control crowded into Revolutionary districts. As early as the end of 1776, committee members were dealing with such problems in the way that traditional corporatist political economy prescribed. They set up manufactories to provide work for people who needed it. They regulated prices and took control of the distribution of scarce goods. They jailed people who violated their orders. After 1776 they found themselves jostling for power not with the institutions of the British empire but rather with American state governments that were proving unequal to the task of controlling the economy.

The committees and what they stood for generated intense opposition among loyalists, of course. But they also provoked a fundamental debate within the Revolutionary coalition, a debate which developed on several levels. It pitted men who had become democrats, enamoured of the people's right to rule, against men who remained Whigs, believing in balance and stability. It pitted plebians just discovering their political identity against members of the old elite, habituated to power. Increasingly, after 1776, it pitted men committed to traditional corporatist views of political economy against believers in the free market. The one position continued to hold that the community had a right to intervene in the use and the disposition of private property; by the late 1770s intervention meant the action of committees and it amounted to a means of lower-class self-defence. The other position held that only an unrestrained market could resolve the country's problems of supply and demand. English thinkers had begun articulating free-market ideology as early as the seventeenth century, and Adam Smith put its case forcefully in *The Wealth of Nations*, published in Britain in 1776. In America the war years saw free-market thought become more and more identified with the mercantile and landed upper class, and with a belief in a complex balance of power rather than a simple direct democracy.[40]

How the elite responded to the popular upheaval varied from state to state.[41] In Pennsylvania they simply lost control in the summer of 1776 and saw the radicals impose a democratic constitution that they loathed. But men of cooler temper rapidly regrouped to oppose the radicals: led by Robert Morris, the Philadelphia merchant who organized Congress's finances, and by James Wilson, judge and legal theorist, they campaigned ceaselessly against the state constitution and for a free market. In 1779 they opposed the revived committee so strongly that a street battle resulted. In Maryland great planters rather than plebians seized control in 1776. They wrote a state constitution whose complicated arrangements were intended to keep the plebians as far as possible from the levers of power. The Boston lawyers and merchants who took the lead in Massachusetts offered two constitutions to the people of their state, one in 1778 and the other in 1780. Both were complex documents, written to establish stability, not to continue participation. The voters rejected the first but accepted the second, and once it was in effect those same leaders imposed a rigid hard-money policy on the state. That policy met the needs of seaport merchants, but ran directly against the interests of western farmers. New York's constitution of 1777 expressly stated that the popular committees had been only a temporary convenience whose necessity was at an end. Between its proclamation — it never was ratified despite the mechanics' demand — and the end of the committee revival, a coalition of landlords, merchants and lawyers did all they could to establish two main principles. One was that despite the committees the constitutional government must be supreme. The other was that the free market must determine the state's economic life.

It was from such disputes that competitive state-level politics developed. Again there was no simple or single way. In New York and Pennsylvania competition brought open partisanship. In Pennsylvania "Constitutionalists" (the radicals) and "Republicans" (the Whigs) confronted each other over the question of the state constitution of 1776. In New York partisanship grew more slowly. The issue at stake was not the shape of the state's government but rather a host of problems of public policy, including the treatment of loyalists, the mode and social effects of taxation, the control of prices, and the distribution of vacant land. In Massachusetts farmers affected by Boston's hard-money policies continued to gather in conventions and to keep the courts closed. They still feared that if the courts opened they would issue writs for the seizure of their farms to pay off debts and taxes. The farmers simply did not have the hard coin in which those debts and taxes were due. Their resistance finally culminated in Shays' Rebellion of 1786, when they briefly took up arms against Boston's policies, and in the next election, when their votes replaced Governor James Bowdoin with John Hancock and brought in a legislature more willing to listen to them.

Meanwhile the planters who wrote Maryland's restrictive state constitution had learned that without plebian consent it simply would not work. Led by Charles Carroll of Carrollton to see "the wisdom of sacrifice," they made massive concessions to popular demands on such questions as taxation and money policy. South Carolina saw intense disputes after independence, among low-country planters, backcountry farmers, and Charleston mechanics and merchants. Only when the introduction of tobacco culture and of massive slavery transformed the backcountry in the image of the lowlands did the state settle down. Even in Virginia, the state least transformed of all, political life was much more open and competitive after 1776 than it had ever been before. All of these changes help explain the fact, noted years ago by Jackson Turner Main, that one consequence of the Revolution was to democratize the state legislatures, bringing into them on a massive scale men who would never have held seats in the provincial assemblies.[42]

In New England, in the mid-Atlantic states, in the Chesapeake, and in the far South alike, men of all sorts disputed over how and in whose interests republican America would run its affairs. Particular disputes might be framed in terms of simple institutions versus complex ones, as in Pennsylvania or Massachusetts. They might be framed in terms of committee power versus regular government, as in New York. They might be framed around the question of soft money versus hard or even, as in Virginia, around the costume of the militia. But they all reflected a tension that ran through the whole continent and the whole era.

All of these disputes culminated in 1787 and 1788 with the struggle over the Federal Constitution. The Constitution replaced the weak continental government that had been established under the Articles of Confederation during the war with a much stronger one, still in operation today. Like New York's constitution of 1777 and the Massachusetts constitution of 1780, it provided for a two-house legislature, a strong executive, and a powerful court system. Like every other stage in the Revolution, its coming was marked by complexity. People entered the Federalist coalition of 1787 and 1788 for just as many reasons as they entered the resistance movement of 1765 and the coalition for independence in 1776. Some were concerned about commerce and trade among the states and with the world; some were worried about America's weakness in a world of power politics; some had evil memories of the difficulty of running the war of independence without an adequate government; some wanted to reorganize American finances. But the men who were central to Federalism — such as Washington, Alexander Hamilton, and James Madison — believed that not only was the central government too weak but also something had gone profoundly wrong in the states. As they looked around them they saw too much soft money, too many men with mud on their boots in power, too much rebellion, too much democracy. They worked to strengthen the central authority for the sake of creating a counter-balance to what they saw at the state level.[43]

It would be wrong, however, to see the Constitution as simply a reaction against everything that had happened since independence. The Federalists mobilized many of the men who had stood in the late 1770s against committee power, simple government and economic corporatism. But they also attracted genuine popular support. In Boston, New York, Philadelphia, Baltimore and Charleston, mechanics paraded behind the banners and symbols of their crafts to celebrate the Constitution. Their enthusiasm was unforced and unfeigned. Twenty years earlier these men had rioted and demonstrated in their anger; now (as the *Appendix* illustrates) they celebrated both what they saw as a solution to America's problems, and the social and political space that they had carved out for themselves. They had left behind their belief that either crowd action or popular committees could solve massive social and economic problems. They were learning to live with free-market economics, and had come to appreciate their interdependence with the people of other states. But most of all, they had gained self-confidence and self-organization, and though they were with the Federalists in 1788 it was because they had thought the questions through for themselves. They would not, in fact, be with them for long. By 1794 they would be lining up politically with the emergent Democratic-Republican party in opposition to the foreign and domestic policies for which Washington and Hamilton had come to stand.[44]

The self-consciousness and political independence of the mechanics encapsulate the difference that the Revolution made to all sorts of people who lived through it. It did not end slavery where slavery was important. It did not make poor Americans into rich ones. America may well have been a less equal society in 1790 than it was in 1765.[45] But the Revolution did strikingly transform the terms on which people dealt with one another, replacing not only monarchy with republicanism but also an elitist political system and political culture with one much more open and democratic. That change happened because people who had found a new political identity in the Revolution forced it to happen.

5: Revolution and Transformation

So complex an event as the Revolution cannot be reduced to any single formula. The configuration of elements and of people and the course of events were simply not the same in Georgia as they were in New Hampshire, or in North Carolina as in New Jersey. But beneath the variety problems common to all thirteen states were working themselves out. One set of problems, the traditional matter of studies of the Revolution, turned on the relationship of America to Britain. The second, which has been this pamphlet's concern, turned on the relationship of ordinary people to the arrangements of power, ideology and privilege that structured their societies. A third, lurking behind the first two, led to the establishment of the political framework within which a liberal, capitalist and industrial society, rapidly expanding to imperial dimensions, would develop in the course of the nineteenth century. The connection between the first and the third is not difficult to see: autonomous development required the end of colonial relations and the establishment of a continental government strong enough to protect it in its infancy.[46] But what is the larger significance of the second set? How were the changes that took in place in political society related to the creation of the United States as we know it?

The answer may lie in a basic congruence between those changes and the central text of American liberalism, James Madison's *Federalist*, no. 10. *The Federalist* was a series of essays jointly written by Madison, Alexander Hamilton and John Jay in 1787 and 1788. Addressed to the people of New York, the essays argued reason after reason why they should accept the new Constitution. In the tenth of those essays Madison addressed the relationship between a republic's size and its prospects for stability. Political thinkers had always maintained that a republic could work only if its citizens had a great deal in common socially and economically and if they acted for the general good rather than to advance their own interests. Madison argued instead that it was possible to have a republic whose citizens would have little in common and who would act for their own selfish reasons.[47] Madison was an ideologue, not a dispassionate analyst. He had a policy to achieve, not simply an essay to publish. But he realized earlier than most Americans that their country was made up of groups of people conscious of their own interests, anxious to control their own world, and willing to struggle in order to do it. Madison saw farmers pouring westward, merchants scrambling for profit, tenants determined to become freeholders, entrepreneurs developing visions of industry, lawyers forming bar associations, and mechanics organizing trade associations. His hope was that in a large republic the political process would yield men capable of the large view. But he realized that the underpinning of the republic would have to lie in self-interest and endless competition, not in self-restraint and high-minded pursuit of the general good. He could not have written the tenth *Federalist* twenty years earlier. The Revolution had been an explosion of involvement, consciousness and self-organization on the part of all sorts of people. They were the people whom Madison observed, and on whose pursuit of self-interest his analysis conferred legitimacy.

The congruence between a social framework comprising many jostling, competing groups and an economic framework based on competitive capitalism is not difficult to perceive. But the Revolution established the pattern of American liberty as well as laying the basis for American capitalism. Part of that pattern is the tradition of individual rights, enshrined in the first ten amendments to the Constitution and enforceable in the courts. But another part of it is the continuing emergence into American society of new self-defined groups, claiming a right to organize and to advance their interests equal to that of any group already established. That is why nineteenth-century factory women struggling against their working conditions, middle-class feminists protesting in 1848 against women's legal subordination, Populist farmers enraged in the 1890s by a marketing system that controlled their lives, and the militants of the Black Panther Party of the 1960s all invoked the heritage of the Revolution to legitimate their own struggles.

In fact, recent writing has shown that even those uses of the Revolution have their roots in the period itself. The Revolution did not bring equality for women, but it did make a significant difference in their lives. Linda Kerber has shown that the notion of "republican motherhood" which emerged during the era was a novel construct in the history of American women. Growing out of the contradiction between the Revolution's rhetoric of liberty and America's reality of sexual subordination, it laid one of the intellectual bases on which an organized self-conscious feminism could begin to take shape. Mary Beth Norton has gone further, finding that the Revolution brought a dramatic shift as women moved from submission to a world over which they had no control to assertion of their own power in that world. At the Revolution's end the women who had lived through it were no longer content to be "good wives," ignorant of the larger world and accepting their exclusion from it. Instead, they were reading newspapers, discussing politics, disputing with the men in their lives, and seeing that their daughters had the best educations possible.[48] Blacks, too, found their lives changed. They were no more a single group than whites, and their experiences varied immensely.

Most were to suffer new forms of slavery, as the cotton South opened up after 1793, but a minority were more fortunate. During the war some escaped to British lines and eventually to Canada; some were manumitted by masters briefly conscious of the claims of liberty; others benefited from emancipation in the North, whether rapid or gradual, in the generation following the Revolution. These new freedmen took the first steps towards making a collective entity of black America — not least, the founding of the Black Protestant churches from which a Martin Luther King would eventually emerge.[49]

The main story of the Revolution, of course, was played out among white males, and what happened in the short run to women and to blacks is peripheral. It is not, however, peripheral to understanding the Revolution's long-range *effects*. The Revolution began with an

The seal of the General Society of Mechanics and Tradesmen of New York City, 1786. More than any other image, this powerful arm and hammer symbolizes the outcome that ordinary people wanted from their Revolution. It represents not only their strength and self-confidence but also their vision of a republican world in which free men would use their energy to produce, not to destroy. The print is taken from a reissue of the membership certificate of the Society.

effort to stave off unwanted changes in how the colonists lived, but it ended by establishing political and social arrangements that led to ceaseless change.[50] In some ways the Federalists of 1787 were trying to put an end to such change when they wrote the Constitution. They were convinced that the surge of ordinary men into public affairs had simply made a mess of American life. That is why they established a government in which, they hoped, men of broad vision, men like themselves, would be in power. They fully expected that a government more distant from the people in spatial and social terms would be less responsive to them in political terms. They wanted to end direct political involvement for the sake of bringing about the legal and economic stability that they believed were necessary to realize their vision of America's future.[51]

But though they created a strong government, they still found that they needed popular involvement to make it work. That is Madison's whole point in the tenth *Federalist*. One might well argue that it was precisely ordinary people's involvement and confidence that they could control their world that gave the federal government its enduring strength as the United States conquered a continent, waged a civil war and industrialized. The Revolution established conditions that would lead within a century to the triumph of corporate capitalism, but it also established conditions in which groups that organized around their own interests could, sometimes, use the power of the state itself to realize those interests. It may well be that America's continuing political stability rests on the interplay between a political order committed at its core to the protection of social arrangements centered on the acquisition and the development of private property, and the fact that large numbers of the republic's citizens have good reason to believe that that political order is their own. Both elements in that interplay were achieved during and as a result of the Revolution.

Appendix:
The Artisans in the Revolution

Throughout the Revolutionary era the artisans (or "mechanics") of America's towns were on the political stage. The changing issues about which they involved themselves, the changing language that they and their spokesmen used, and the changing means they employed to express their concerns show graphically how one group changed the terms of its involvement in American society during the Revolution.

The artisans were not a working class in the modern sense of the term. Though they worked with their hands, producing goods for others to buy and use, they were not employees in capitalist enterprises. Rather, they did their work in small shops, each presided over by a master of the trade, each including independent journeymen hired for a term as well as apprentices learning how it was done. Journeymen and apprentices alike looked forward to becoming masters themselves. Artisans formed their identities in terms of their crafts, and during the Revolution they formed those identities in terms of a claim that they should enjoy political rights equal to those of anyone else. We can watch that claim taking shape, as first they asserted their right to involvement in the movement, then realized their power to speak out in their own interest, and finally took a central part in the making of the Republic.

Artisan involvement first became an issue during the boycott of British goods with which the colonies resisted the Townshend taxes. The non-importation movement was good for American mechanics, because it assured that there would be a market for their own goods. But when non-importation began to crumble in 1770, artisans found that they and their merchant allies had different views. For the merchants, it meant, at last, a chance to resume their businesses, and they claimed the right to decide for themselves when they would do it. For the tradesmen it meant competition once again from British goods, and they claimed a say in whether the boycott should end. Here is how one Philadelphia broadside of 1770, signed "A Tradesman," made the case:

> And will you suffer the Credit and Liberties of the Province of Pennsylvania to be sacrificed to the Interests of a few Merchants in Philadephia? Shall the GRAND QUESTION, whether America shall be free or not, be determined by a few Men, whose Support and Importance must always be in Proportion to the Distresses of our Country? ... In determining Questions of such great Consequence, the Consent of the Majority of the Tradesmen, Farmers and other Freemen ... should have been obtained .... The Tradesmen who have suffered

> by the Non-Importation Agreement are but few, when compared to the Number of those who have received great Benefit from it . . . . I conjure you by the Love you bear to yourselves — to your country — to your posterity — and above all by the Homage you owe to HUMAN LIBERTY, not to surrender . . . but to assert your Freedom at the Expence of your Fortunes and your Blood.[52]

During the Independence crisis artisans openly assumed a separate station in political life. In Worcester, Massachusetts, blacksmiths resolved not to "do or perform, any blacksmith's work or business . . . for any person or persons whom we esteem enemies to this country" and recommended "to all denominations of artificers that they call meetings of their respective craftsmen . . . and enter into associations and agreements" to do the same.[53] The smiths were acting for the common cause, but by the end of the 1770s, as inflation ravaged the American economy, other mechanics were looking to their own interests. In Philadelphia the leather trades decided in 1779 that they wanted an end to public efforts to control the market, and they told other Pennsylvanians why:

> The committee . . . hint that their fixing the prices of our commodities first, was in a great measure to give us "the preference of setting the first example as a rule for other trades, for though only one was mentioned, all were intentionally and inclusively regulated." And we would gladly have made that honour our own, by a compliance, did not we see . . . that any partial regulation of any number of articles would answer no end but that of destroying the tradesman whose prices are limited, and . . . leaving the country in absolute want of those articles.[54]

Many artisans would not have agreed with the leatherworkers' insistence that the free market should determine the price of all goods. But they would have endorsed emphatically the fact that the tanners and curriers and shoemakers were thinking for themselves, calculating their own interests. The many artisans, all over America, who supported the Federal Constitution in 1787 and 1788 were doing the same thing. Here is a meeting of Boston tradesmen, announcing its position:

> It is our opinion, if said Constitution should be adopted . . . Trade and Navigation will revive and increase, employ and subsistence will be afforded to many of our Townsmen, who are now suffering from want of the necessaries of life; that it will promote industry and morality, render us respectable as a nation; and procure us all the blessings to which we are entitled from the natural wealth of our country, our capacity for improvement, from our industry, our freedom and independence.[55]

Mechanics throughout the country showed that they agreed when they joined in massive parades to celebrate as their states declared ratification. In Charleston, in New York, in Philadelphia, in Baltimore, in Boston and in lesser towns as well, men marched behind the banners of their crafts. Carrying their tools, and even pulling floats on which some of their number were putting them to use, they displayed slogans that proclaimed their republican American identity and their pride in themselves. "Both Buildings and Rulers Are the Work of Our Hands," announced the Philadelphia bricklayers. "Time Rules All Things," proclaimed the clockmakers. "By Hammer and Hand, All Arts Do Stand," read the banner of the smiths. "May Our Country Never Want Bread," said the bakers.[56]

Twenty years earlier, such parades would not have been possible. They were patriotic celebrations, proclaiming the delight of people who had once been colonial subjects and had now become republican citizens. But they were also celebrations of the self, proclaiming the pride in being what they were that the artisans had built as they waged their Revolution.

Guide to Further Reading

Readers requiring a narrative introduction to the Revolution should turn to one of the following one-volume studies written specifically to introduce the subject: Esmond Wright, *Fabric of Freedom, 1763-1800* (London: Macmillan, 1965; rev. edn., New York: Hill & Wang, 1978); Edmund S. Morgan, *The Birth of the Republic, 1763-1789* (Chicago: Univ. of Chicago Press, 1956); and J.R. Pole, *Foundations of American Independence, 1763-1815* (Indianapolis: Bobbs-Merrill, 1972; London: Fontana-Collins, 1973).

Those who wish to explore the Revolution more widely and deeply are presented with two possible reading strategies. One is to begin with the classics and work through the historiography to the present day. Two anthologies can serve as starting places for the reader following this route. One is Jack P. Greene, ed., *The Reinterpretation of the American Revolution, 1763-1789* (New York: Harper & Row, 1968), which contains a superb bibliographical essay and an excellent collection of mid-twentieth-century essays and excerpts. The other is Edmund S. Morgan, ed., *The American Revolution: Two Centuries of Interpretation* (Englewood Cliffs, N.J.: Prentice-Hall, 1965), which has selections from eighteenth, nineteenth and twentieth-century writers. Selections from the writings of the Imperial and the Progressive historians, not included in either Greene or Morgan, can be found in Esmond Wright, ed., *Causes and Consequences of the American Revolution* (Chicago: Quadrangle, 1966). All these anthologies provide samples from the original major works which the reader can move on to as he or she chooses.

The other reading strategy is to begin with the contemporary debate. In that case, a starting place can be found in Pauline Maier, *From Resistance to Revolution: Colonial Radicals and the Development of American Opposition to Britain, 1765-1776* (1972),[11]* and in the anthology edited by Alfred F. Young entitled *The American Revolution: Explorations in the History of American Radicalism* (1976).[32]* Maier and the writers in the Young book consider many of the same problems and much of the same evidence, but with different points of view, emphases and conclusions. The contrasts between them in many ways pose the framework for contemporary discussion.

The approach to the Revolution from the point of view of political culture receives its central statement in Bernard Bailyn, *The Ideological Origins of the American Revolution* (1967).[12] The origins of that culture are considered at length in J.G.A. Pocock, *The Machiavellian Moment: Florentine Political Thought and the Atlantic Republican Tradition* (1975).[10] What became of it after independence is discussed at equal length — and most revealingly — in Gordon S. Wood, *The Creation of the*

---

* For full bibliographical details, see the appropriate reference in the Notes, as indicated.

American Republic, 1776-1787 (1969).[11] J.R. Pole writes within much the same framework in *Political Repesentation in England and the Origins of the American Republic* (1966),[30] which incorporates detailed studies of the key states of Pennsylvania, Virginia and Massachusetts. Somewhat older, but still useful, is Clinton Rossiter, *Seedtime of the Republic* (1953).[10] The link between ideas and action is considered in Maier, *From Resistance to Revolution*, in Edmund S. and Helen M. Morgan, *The Stamp Act Crisis: Prologue to Revolution* (Chapel Hill: Univ. of North Carolina Press, 1953), and, from a different viewpoint, in Eric Foner, *Tom Paine and Revolutionary America* (1976).[38]

A number of scholars have considered the social, as opposed to intellectual background to the Revolution. Jack P. Greene has written on it in a number of places, but most succinctly in his Harmsworth inaugural lecture at Oxford, *All Men are Created Equal: Some Reflections on the Character of the American Revolution* (Oxford: Clarendon Press, 1976). Richard Hofstadter deals with it in *America at 1750: A Social Portrait* (New York: Knopf, 1971), as does Jackson Turner Main in *The Social Structure of Revolutionary America* (1965)[13] and Kenneth Lockridge in *Settlement and Unsettlement in Early America* (Cambridge, England: Cambridge UP, 1981). Perhaps the most sophisticated single statement is James A. Henretta, *The Evolution of American Society, 1700-1815* (1973),[17] which should be supplemented by his essay "Families and Farms: *Mentalité* in Pre-Industrial America," *William and Mary Quarterly*, **35** (1978), 3-32, and by Michael Merrill, "Cash is Good to Eat: Self-Sufficiency and Exchange in the Rural Economy of the United States," *Radical History Review*, no. 4 (1977), 42-71.

The testing ground for the broad generalizations in these studies is to be found in analyses of communities and states. One of the most easily grasped, yet most sophisticated, is Robert Gross's *The Minutemen and Their World* (1976),[27] a study of Concord, Massachusetts. A number of other studies are roughly congruent with Gross's approach, likewise finding significant social tensions within the Revolutionary movement. These include, working from north to south, the following: Richard L. Bushman, *From Puritan to Yankee* (1967),[31] on Connecticut; Edward Countryman, *A People in Revolution, 1760-1790* (1981),[15] on New York; Rhys Isaac, *The Transformation of Virginia, 1740-1790* (1982);[14] Ronald Hoffman, *A Spirit of Dissension* (1974),[32] on Maryland; and Jerome J. Nadelhaft, *The Disorders of War: The Revolution in South Carolina* (1981).[34] Gary B. Nash, *The Urban Crucible* (1979)[14] discusses and compares developments in the three major cities.

Against these, however, should be read studies which do not find that social tensions contributed significantly to the Revolutionary movement. The most seminal is Robert E. Brown, *Middle-Class Democracy and the Revolution in Massachusetts* (1955).[6] This can be read in conjunction with Patricia U. Bonomi, *A Factious People: Politics and*

Society in Colonial New York (1971);[16] Sung Bok Kim, *Landlord and Tenant in Colonial New York: Manorial Society, 1664-1775* (Chapel Hill: Univ. of North Carolina Press, 1978); Jere R. Daniell, *Experiment in Republicanism: New Hampshire Politics and the American Revolution, 1741-1794* (Cambridge, Mass.: Harvard UP, 1970); and A. Roger Ekirch, *"Poor Carolina": Politics and Society in Colonial North Carolina, 1729-1776* (1981).[16] A view of urban development that conflicts with Nash's can be found in G.B. Warden, "Inequality and Instability in Eighteenth-Century Boston: A Reappraisal," *Journal of Interdisciplinary History*, **6** (1975-76), 585-620. In all of these studies, conflict is ascribed to tensions within middle-class society rather than — as in this pamphlet — to the working-out of fundamental contradictions.

The radicals of the Revolution are considered in a number of places. Pauline Maier supplements *From Resistance to Revolution* (1972)[11] with her *The Old Revolutionaries: Political Lives in the Age of Samuel Adams* (1980).[25] Eric Foner's study of *Tom Paine and Revolutionary America* (1976)[38] places its subject firmly in social context. The Revolutionary committees are considered, in different ways, not only in Gordon Wood's *Creation of the American Republic*[11] and Countryman's *A People in Revolution*,[15] but also in Richard D. Brown, *Revolutionary Politics in Massachusetts: The Boston Committee of Correspondence and the Towns, 1772-1774* (Cambridge, Mass.: Harvard UP, 1970), and Richard Alan Ryerson, *The Revolution is Now Begun: The Radical Committees of Philadelphia, 1765-1776* (1978).[35] Crowd action is a major subject of the books by Maier, Foner, Nash, Countryman, Ekirch, Bonomi and Kim noted above, but the most important study is Dirk Hoerder, *Crowd Action in Revolutionary Massachusetts, 1765-1780* (1977).[26]

Three main studies now encompass the debate on women and the Revolution. They are: Joan Hoff Wilson, "The Illusion of Change: Women and the American Revolution," in Young, ed., *The American Revolution*,[32] pp. 383-445; Mary Beth Norton, *Liberty's Daughters: The Revolutionary Experience of American Women, 1750-1800* (1980);[18] and Linda Kerber, *Women of the Republic: Intellect and Ideology in Revolutinary America* (1980).[48] The superb anthology edited by Ira Berlin and Ronald Hoffman, *Slavery and Freedom in the Age of the American Revolution* (1983),[49] represents the most advanced thinking on the experience of Black Americans in the era. The subject is discussed at length in David Brion Davis, *The Problem of Slavery in the Age of Revolution, 1770-1823* (Ithaca: Cornell UP, 1975), Duncan J. MacLeod, *Slavery, Race and the American Revolution* (Cambridge, England: Cambridge UP, 1974) and Benjamin Quarles, *The Negro in the American Revolution* (Chapel Hill: Univ. of North Carolina Press, 1961).

It is perhaps not surprising, given the attention that modern scholarship has paid to the ideology and the social process of the

Revolution, that very little work has considered the American colonies in the light of contemporary debates on colonialism, underdevelopment and dependency. There is nothing to match the analysis of Stanley and Barbara Stein in *The Colonial Heritage of Latin America: Essays on Eocnomic Dependence in Perspective* (New York: Oxford UP, 1970). Three recent books, however, present a suggestive start, in different ways: Paul G.E. Clemens, *The Atlantic Economy and Colonial Maryland's Eastern Shore: From Tobacco to Grain* (Ithaca: Cornell UP, 1980); Joseph A. Ernst, *Money and Politics in America, 1755-1775: A Study in the Currency Act of 1764 and the Political Economy of Revolution* (Chapel Hill: Univ. of North Carolina Press, 1973), and Michael Kammen, *Empire and Interest: The American Colonies and the Politics of Mercantilism* (Philadelphia: Lippincott, 1970). Possibilities for further study along these lines are discussed in Edward Countryman and Susan Deans, "Independence and Revolution in the Americas: A Project for Comparative Study" (1983).[46] The problem of unequal colonial relations lurks behind the rich analysis in Edmund S. Morgan, *American Slavery, American Freedom: The Ordeal of Colonial Virginia* (New York: Norton, 1975).

The Bicentennial decade produced a sizable number of excellent anthologies on the Revolution. In addition to Alfred F. Young's *The American Revolution* (1976),[32] these include: Stephen G. Kurtz and James H. Hutson, eds., *Essays on the American Revolution* (1973);[12] Erich Angermann et al., eds., *New Wine in Old Skins: A Comparative View of Socio-Political Structures and Values Affecting the American Revolution* (1976);[39] Jack P. Greene and Pauline Maier, eds., *Interdisciplinary Studies of the American Revolution* (Beverly Hills: Sage, 1976); Richard Maxwell Brown and Don E. Fehrenbacher, eds., *Tradition, Conflict and Modernization: Perspectives on the American Revolution* (1977);[24] Richard M. Jellison, ed., *Society, Freedom and Conscience: The American Revolution in Virginia, Massachusetts and New York* (1976);[27] and Ronald Hoffman and Peter J. Albert, eds., *Sovereign States in an Age of Uncertainty* (1982).[41]

Finally, Alfred F. Young traces the Revolutionary experience of one Boston shoemaker in his prize-winning essay "George Robert Twelves Hewes: A Boston Shoemaker and the Memory of the American Revolution," *William and Mary Quarterly*, **38** (1981), 561-623. Hewes's career led him through so many of the Revolution's facets and transformations that it comes as close as anyone's to epitomizing what the era meant for Everyman.

Notes

1. E.g., Staughton Lynd, "Abraham Yates's History of the Movement for the United States Constitution," in his *Class Conflict, Slavery and the United States Constitution* (Indianapolis: Bobbs-Merrill, 1967), pp. 217-46.
2. George Bancroft, *History of the United States*, 6 vols. (1834-76; rev. edn., N.Y.: Appleton, 1883-85).
3. For the most succinct statements, see Charles M.Andrews, *Colonial Background of the American Revolution* (New Haven: Yale UP, 1924) and L.H. Gipson, "The American Revolution as an Aftermath of the Great War for Empire, 1754-1763," *Political Science Quarterly*, **65** (1950), 86-104.
4. Carl L. Becker, *The History of Political Parties in the Province of New York, 1760-1776* (Madison: Univ. of Wisconsin Press, 1909).
5. Charles A. Beard, *An Economic Interpretation of the Constitution of the United States* (N.Y.: Macmillan, 1913).
6. The most important is Robert E. Brown, *Middle-Class Democracy and the Revolution in Massachusetts* (Ithaca: Cornell UP, 1955).
7. Forrest McDonald, *We the People: The Economic Origins of the Constitution* (Chicago: Univ. of Chicago Press, 1958).
8. Carl L. Becker, *The Declaration of Independence* (New York: Knopf, 1922).
9. E.S. Morgan, "Colonial Ideas of Parliamentary Power, 1764-66," *William and Mary Quarterly*, **5** (1948), 311-41.
10. Clinton Rossiter, *Seedtime of the Republic* (N.Y.: Harcourt, Brace and World, 1953); D.G. Adair, "Experience Must Be Our Only Guide: History, Democratic Theory, and the United States Constitution," in Ray Allen Billington, ed., *The Reinterpretation of Early American History: Essays in Honor of John Edwin Pomfret* (San Marino, Cal.: Huntington Library, 1966); Cecelia Kenyon, ed., *The Antifederalists* (Indianapolis: Bobbs-Merrill, 1966); J.G.A. Pocock, *The Machiavellian Moment: Florentine Political Thought and the Atlantic Republican Tradition* (Princeton, N.J.: Princeton UP, 1975).
11. Gordon S. Wood, *The Creation of the American Republic, 1776-1787* (Chapel Hill: Univ. of North Carolina Press, 1969); Pauline Maier, *From Resistance to Revolution: Colonial Radicals and the Development of American Opposition to Britian, 1765-1776* (N.Y.: Knopf, 1972).
12. See esp. Bernard Bailyn, *The Ideological Origins of the American Revolution* (Cambridge, Mass.: Harvard UP, 1967); and, for a summary of the "ideological" interpretation, his essay on "The Central Themes of the American Revolution," in Stephen G. Kurtz and James H. Hutson, eds., *Essays on the American Revolution* (Chapel Hill: Univ. of North Carolina Press, 1973), pp. 3-31.
13. Merrill Jensen, *The Articles of Confederation* (Madison: Univ. of Wisconsin Press, 1940), *The New Nation: A History of the United States During the Confederation, 1781-1789* (N.Y.: Knopf, 1950), *The Founding of a Nation: A History of the American Revolution, 1763-1776* (N.Y.: Oxford UP, 1968). For a summary of Main's position, see his *The Social Structure of Revolutionary America* (Princeton, N.J.: Princeton UP, 1965).
14. Gary B. Nash, *The Urban Crucible: Social Change, Political Consciousness, and the Origins of the American Revolution* (Cambridge, Mass.: Harvard UP, 1979); Rhys Isaac, *The Transformation of Virginia, 1740-1790* (Chapel Hill: Univ. of North Carolina Press, 1982).

15. Edward Countryman, *A People in Revolution: The American Revolution and Political Society In New York, 1760-1790* (Baltimore: John Hopkins UP, 1981).

16. For an overview of colonial political life, see Bernard Bailyn, *The Origins of American Politics* (N.Y.: Vintage, 1970). This chapter draws heavily on the following state studies, in rough geographical order: Michael Zuckerman, "The Social Context of Democracy in Massachusetts," *William and Mary Quarterly*, **25** (1968), 523-44, reprinted in Stanley N. Katz, ed., *Colonial America: Essays in Politics and Social Development* (Boston: Little, Brown, 1971), pp. 466-91; Patricia U. Bonomi, *A Factious People: Politics and Society in Colonial New York* (N.Y.: Columbia UP, 1971), and Countryman, *A People In Revolution*, ch. 3; Gary B. Nash, *Quakers and Politics: Pennsylvania, 1681-1726* (Princeton, N.J.: Princeton UP, 1968); Isaac, *Transformation of Virginia*; A. Roger Ekirch, *"Poor Carolina": Politics and Society in Colonial North Carolina, 1729-1776* (Chapel Hill: Univ. of North Carolina Press, 1981); R.M. Weir, "'The Harmony We Were Famous For': An Interpretation of Pre-Revolutionary South Carolina Politics," *William and Mary Quarterly* **26**, (1969), 473-501.

17. James A. Henretta, *The Evolution of American Society, 1700-1815: An Interdisciplinary Analysis* (N.Y.: Heath, 1973).

18. Laurel Thatcher Ulrich, *Good Wives: Image and Reality in the Lives of Women in Northern New England, 1650-1750* (N.Y.: Knopf, 1982); Mary Beth Norton, *Liberty's Daughters: The Revolutionary Experience of American Women, 1750-1800* (Boston: Little, Brown, 1980), Part 1.

19. Nash, *Urban Crucible*, pp. 233-63, 312-38.

20. Kenneth Lockridge, "Land, Population and the Evolution of New England Society, 1630-1790," *Past & Present*, No. 39 (1968), 62-80, reprinted with an afterthought in Katz, *Colonial America*, pp. 466-91.

21. For the most recent analysis of the administration of the empire, see James A. Henretta, *"Salutary Neglect": Colonial Administration Under the Duke of Newcastle* (Princeton, N.J.: Princeton UP, 1972); also Jack P. Greene, "An Uneasy Connection: An Analysis of the Preconditions of the American Revolution," in Kurtz and Hutson, eds., *Essays on the Revolution*, pp. 32-80. For the colonial elite, see Stanley N. Katz, *Newcastle's New York: Anglo-American Politics, 1732-1753* (Cambridge, Mass.: Harvard UP, 1968); Charles S. Sydnor, *Gentlemen Freeholders: Political Practices in Washington's Virginia* (Chapel Hill: Univ. of North Carolina Press, 1952).

22. Pauline Maier, "Popular Uprisings and Civil Authority in Eighteenth-Century America," *William and Mary Quarterly*, **27** (1970), 3-35, and in her *From Resistance to Revolution*, ch.1; Jesse Lemisch, "Jack Tar in the Streets: Merchant Seamen in the Politics of Revolutionary America," *William and Mary Quarterly*, **25** (1968), 371-407.

23. Nash, pp. 129-36; Countryman, pp. 56-58; E.P. Thompson, "The Moral Economy of the English Crowd in the Eighteenth Century," *Past & Present*, No. 50 (1971), 76-136.

24. For an overview, see R.M. Brown, "Back Country Rebellions and the Homestead Ethic in America, 1740-1799," in Richard Maxwell Brown and Don E. Fehrenbacher, eds., *Tradition, Conflict and Modernization: Perspectives on the American Revolution* (N.Y.: Academic Press, 1977).

25. Maier, *From Resistance to Revolution* and *The Old Revolutionaries: Political Lives in the Age of Samuel Adams* (N.Y.: Knopf, 1980).

26. Dirk Hoerder, *Crowd Action in Revolutionary Massachusetts, 1765-1780* (N.Y.: Academic Press, 1977), ch.2; Maier, *From Resistance to Revolution*, ch.3; Countryman, ch.2.

27. R.L. Bushman, "Massachusetts Farmers and the Revolution," in Richard M. Jellison, ed., *Society, Freedom and Conscience: The American Revolution in Virginia, Massachusetts and New York* (N.Y.: Norton, 1976); Richard D. Brown, *Revolutionary Politics in Massachusetts: The Boston Committee of Correspondence and the Towns, 1772-1774* (Cambridge, Mass.: Harvard UP, 1970); Robert A. Gross, *The Minutemen and Their World* (N.Y.: Hill & Wang, 1976). See also John M. Murrin's creative "Review Essay" on the early New England social literature, *History and Theory*, **11** (1972), 226-75.

28. For an argument that the era saw a general social crisis in rural America, see Henretta, *Evolution of American Society*, ch.4.

29. Countryman, chs.2, 4, 5.

30. J.R. Pole, *Political Representation in England and the Origins of the American Republic* (London: Macmillan, 1966), pp. 285, 294-95.

31. Isaac, *Transformation of Virginia*, chs. 7-11; E.J. Hobsbawm, *Primitive Rebels: Studies in Archaic Forms of Social Movement in the 19th and 20th Centuries* (Manchester: Manchester UP, 1959). For the impact of the Great Awakening, see Richard L. Bushman, *From Puritan to Yankee: Character and the Social Order in Connecticut, 1680-1775* (Cambridge, Mass.: Harvard UP, 1967).

32. J.P. Whittenburg, "Planters, Merchants and Lawyers: Social Change and the Origins of the North Carolina Regulation," *William and Mary Quarterly*, **34** (1977), 215-38; Ronald Hoffman, *A Spirit of Dissension: Economics, Politics and the Revolution in Maryland* (Baltimore: Johns Hopkins UP, 1973); Edward Countryman, "'Out of the Bounds of the Law': Northern Land Rioters in the Eighteenth Century," in Alfred F. Young, ed., *The American Revolution: Explorations in the History of American Radicalism* (DeKalb, Ill.: Northern Illinois UP, 1976),pp. 37-69; Stephen A. Marini, *Radical Sects of Revolutionary New England* (Cambridge, Mass.: Harvard UP, 1982).

33. For the continuity argument, see Clinton Rossiter, *The First American Revolution: The American Colonies on the Eve of Independence* (N.Y.: Harcourt, Brace and World, 1956); Daniel J. Boorstin, *The Genius of American Politics* (Chicago: Univ. of Chicago Press, 1953); and Benjamin F. Wright, *Consensus and Continuity, 1776-1787* (Boston: Boston UP, 1958).

34. Isaac, ch.11; Jerome J. Nadelhaft, *The Disorders of War: The Revolution in South Carolina* (Orono, Maine: Univ. of Maine Press, 1981), ch.1.

35. Richard A. Ryerson, *The Revolution is Now Begun: The Radical Committees of Philadelphia, 1765-1776* (Philadelphia: Univ. of Pennsylvania Press, 1978).

36. Countryman, *A People In Revolution*, pp. 131-60.

37. Ibid.; Ryerson, *The Revolution is Now Begun*, pp. 122-24.

38. Eric Foner, *Tom Paine and Revolutionary America* (N.Y.: Oxford UP, 1976).

39. Countryman, pp. 162-63. See also Ryerson, chs.4, 8; and Dirk Hoerder, "Socio-Political Structures and Popular Ideology, 1750s-1780s," in Erich Angermann et al., eds., *New Wine in Old Skins: A Comparative View of Socio-Political Structures and Values Affecting the American Revolution* (Stuttgart: Ernst Klett, 1976), pp. 41-65.

40. See Foner, esp. ch.5, and Countryman, ch.6. For the origins of free-market thought, see Joyce O. Appleby, *Economic Thought and Ideology in Seventeenth-Century*

England (Princeton, N.J.: Princeton UP, 1978); C.B. MacPherson, *The Political Theory of Possessive Individualism: Hobbes to Locke* (Oxford: Clarendon Press, 1962).

41. The following paragraphs draw heavily on the following state studies: R.A. Ryerson, "Republican Theory and Partisan Reality in Revolutionary Pennsylvania: Toward a New View of the Constitutionalist Party," in Ronald Hoffman and Peter J. Albert, eds., *Sovereign States in an Age of Uncertainty* (Charlottesville: Univ. Press of Virginia, 1982), pp. 95-133; for Maryland, Hoffman, *A Spirit of Dissension*, chs.8, 9; for Massachusetts, David P. Szatmary, *Shays' Rebellion: The Making of an Agrarian Insurrection* (Amherst: Univ. of Massachusetts Press, 1980), and Pole, *Political Representation*, pp. 226-43; Countryman, chs. 7-9, on New York, and Isaac on Virginia; and, for South Carolina, Nadelhaft, *The Disorders of War*.

42. J.T. Main, "Government by the People: The American Revolution and the Democratization of the Legislatures," *William and Mary Quarterly*, **23** (1966), 391-407. See also Main's *Political Parties Before The Constitution* (Chapel Hill: Univ. of North Carolina Press, 1973).

43. Wood, *Creation of the American Republic*, Parts 4 and 5.

44. Countryman, chs. 9 and 10; Alfred F. Young, *The Democratic Republicans of New York: the Origins, 1763-1797* (Chapel Hill: Univ. of North Carolina Press), pp. 101, 387. For the artisans' progress from protest through self-assertion to active citizenship, see the materials in the *Appendix*.

45. See Alan Kulikoff, "The Progress of Inequality in Revolutionary Boston," *William and Mary Quarterly*, **28** (1971), 375-412.

46. See Edward Countryman and Susan Deans, "Independence and Revolution in the Americas: A Project for Comparative Study," *Radical History Review*, No. 27 (1983), 144-71.

47. D.G. Adair, "That Politics May Be Reduced to a Science: David Hume, James Madison and the Tenth *Federalist*," *Huntington Library Quarterly*, **20** (1957), 343-60.

48. Linda K. Kerber, *Women of the Republic: Intellect and Ideology in Revolutionary America* (Chapel Hill: Univ. of North Carolina Press, 1980); Norton, *Liberty's Daughters*.

49. Ira Berlin and Ronald Hoffman, eds., *Slavery and Freedom in the Age of the American Revolution* (Charlottesville: Univ. Press of Virginia, 1983).

50. For such an argument in the context of a particular community, see Gross, *The Minutemen and Their World*.

51. Wood, *Creation of the American Republic*, ch.12.

52. "A Tradesman," broadside (Philadelphia, 1770), no. 11892 in Charles Evans, *American Bibliography: A Chronological Dictionary of All Books, Pamphlets and Periodical Publications Printed in the United States of America, 1639-1800*, 14 vols. (Chicago, 1903-59).

53. Blacksmiths' minutes, 8 Sept., 8 Nov. 1774, Massachusetts Collection, American Antiquarian Society, Worcester, Mass.

54. "Tanners, Curriers and Cordwainers to the Inhabitants of Pennsylvania," broadside (Philadelphia, 1779), Evans no. 16547.

55. Boston *Independent Chronicle*, 13 Dec. 1787.

56. *Pennsylvania Gazette*, reported in *Connecticut Courant*, 21 July 1788.

BAAS PAMPHLETS IN AMERICAN STUDIES

1. **SLAVERY**
   by Peter J. Parish
2. **PROGRESSIVISM**
   by J.A. Thompson
3. **THE PRESIDENT AND THE SUPREME COURT: NEW DEAL TO WATERGATE**
   by John D. Lees
4. **THE METROPOLITAN MOSAIC: PROBLEMS OF THE CONTEMPORARY CITY**
   by Philip Davies
5. **THE COMIC SELF IN POST-WAR AMERICAN FICTION**
   by Stan Smith
6. **THE AMERICAN DREAM**
   by Robert H. Fossum and John K. Roth
7. **THE WELFARE STATE IN AMERICA, 1930-1980**
   by James T. Patterson
8. **MODERN INDIANS: NATIVE AMERICANS IN THE TWENTIETH CENTURY**
   by David Murray
9. **THE EXPATRIATE TRADITION IN AMERICAN LITERATURE**
   by Malcolm Bradbury
10. **THE IMMIGRANT EXPERIENCE IN AMERICAN LITERATURE**
    by Edward. A. Abramson
11. **BLACK AMERICAN FICTION SINCE RICHARD WRIGHT**
    by A. Robert Lee
12. **AMERICAN PHOTOGRAPHY**
    by Mick Gidley
13. **THE PEOPLE'S AMERICAN REVOLUTION**
    by Edward Countryman

Pamphlets may be purchased from BAAS Pamphlets, c/o The Historical Association, 59a Kennington Park Road, London SE11 4JH, England.